Cover to Cover Bible Study

C000006690

7 Sessions for Homegroup
and Personal Use

The
Holy Spirit

Understanding and experiencing Him

Selwyn Hughes
WITH IAN SEWTER

Contents

Contents

Introduction

The subject of this *Cover to Cover* Bible study guide
is the ministry and Person of the Holy Spirit, who some
describe as 'the shy member of the Trinity'. The reason
He is referred to as 'shy' is because He appears reluctant
to talk about Himself. The One who inspires the Bible
keeps Himself very much in the background. In reality
the Holy Spirit is anything but shy. His reticence about
focusing on Himself is not due to shyness but to His
commitment to turning the spotlight on the face of Christ,
and revealing to us the way of salvation through faith in
His sacrificial death on the cross for our sins.

Despite the Holy Spirit's reticence, the Bible does contain
a wealth of revelation about Him. A lack of understanding of the Person and ministry of the Holy Spirit
will impoverish our Christian faith and could stunt our
spiritual growth. To understand more about Him is to
understand more about God Himself and that knowledge
will strengthen our faith and make us more spiritually
fruitful.

One of the problems facing us as Christians when we
come to discuss the Holy Spirit is the fact that the Church
is greatly divided over the issue of how He operates and
functions in the life of believers. The Church is however
united on one thing – Christianity is a faith in which the
Holy Spirit plays a prominent part. The benediction most
used in Christian circles includes the phrase, 'The grace
of the Lord Jesus Christ, and the love of God, and the
fellowship of the Holy Spirit be with you all.' Note the
steps: the grace of Jesus Christ, introduces you to the love
of God, which results in you enjoying the fellowship of
the Holy Spirit. Grace and love are designed to lead
you into a relationship with the Holy Spirit and that
relationship is for all. It is the destiny of every Christian

to understand who the Holy Spirit is and experience His companionship. Anything less is less than God intended. In faith we must expect Jesus to fulfil His promise when He said that He would send another just like Himself who would be with us for ever (John 14:16).

The Holy Spirit seeks to draw out of us all the potential which God has built into us and is continually at work developing us into the kind of persons God sees us to be. He stimulates us to pray, and prays in us and through us. He brings hidden things to light in our souls and seeks to rid us of all sin. The divine Counsellor shines the laser beam of knowledge and wisdom through the fog that sometimes surrounds us and guides us in ways of which we are both conscious and unconscious along the path He wants us to take. He teaches us as no other could and leads us in the thing our hearts were built for – truth. The heavenly Dove broods over our lives to bring beauty and order into our dark empty worlds. He comforts us whenever we are in need of solace, and strengthens our hearts to go on even though we have no clear answers to our questions. The Holy Spirit longs to produce His fruit in our lives and bestow us with gifts and abilities to build up the Body of Christ and reach out to others with the message of God's love. When we open up to Him, to depend on Him and consult Him, we receive the love, wisdom and spiritual sustenance we need to live effectively and dynamically for Christ. The Church of Jesus Christ in this age must lay hold on the truth of the Spirit with greater determination than ever for, as an old Welsh saying puts it: *Heb Ysbryd Glan – Heb Ddim –* 'Without the Spirit – without anything.' We might say, 'With the Spirit – with everything!' We need the Holy Spirit's fire personally for our intellect, emotions and will, and also for our homes, our churches, our businesses and our nations.

At the end of this study we shall not only have a deeper understanding of the Person and work of the Holy Spirit, but also a closer communion with Him. The creeds simply say, 'I believe in the Holy Spirit', but much more than mere belief is needed. Belief must become experience. It is not enough to believe in the doctrine of the Spirit, we must experience Him in all His fullness. That is the challenge that lies before us – to move from belief to experience, from knowing about Him to actually knowing Him personally. We study the fruit of the Spirit that we might be more fruitful; we study the gifts of the Spirit that we might be more effective; and we study the Person and fullness of the Spirit that we might lead a more Spirit-filled life.

WEEK 1

The Person of the Holy Spirit

Opening Icebreaker

What are the characteristics of personality? For example, what distinguishes a person from a robot, animal, mineral or vegetable?

Bible Readings

- Matthew 28:19
- John 14:16–17, 26
- Acts 5:1–4; 13:1–4
- 2 Corinthians 13:14
- Ephesians 4:30

Opening Our Eyes

The Holy Spirit is not merely an influence or impersonal power but is actually a divine Person. That is why, when we talk about Him, we must refer to Him as 'He' and not 'it'. Passages such as Matthew 28:19 and 2 Corinthians 13:14 speak of the Father, Son and Holy Spirit in the same sentence. In this context it would be inconsistent to think of the Father and Son as Persons but the Holy Spirit as an influence. In John's Gospel, although the word 'spirit' is in the neuter gender, Jesus Himself used personal pronouns when He spoke of the Holy Spirit (eg John 14:16–17, 26; 15:26; 16:7–14). The Holy Spirit is not the personification of an influence, the sense of fellowship Christians experience when they get together or even spiritual enthusiasm. He is a person in the same way that you and I are persons – only of course much more so. He is an individual with intelligence, knowledge, wisdom, sympathy and so on. He can speak, rejoice, love, whisper and can be hurt in the same way a close friend can be hurt.

The Bible clearly reveals the Holy Spirit to have emotions, thoughts and an individual will to make decisions. Ephesians 4:30 in the Amplified Bible says, 'do not grieve the Holy Spirit of God (do not offend, or vex or sadden Him)'. In a similar way, Acts 5 shows that He can be lied to and Hebrews 10:29 that He can be insulted. We cannot insult or lie to an influence, but the Holy Spirit can be saddened and even insulted by our attitudes and actions. Romans 8:27 refers to the 'mind of the Spirit' while Acts 15:28 records 'It seemed good to the Holy Spirit and to us.' Here we have an indication of the Holy Spirit's ability to think and make decisions. This is more clearly stated in 1 Corinthians 12:11 where He chooses who will receive His various gifts. The Holy Spirit is shown to communicate, in passages such as Acts 13 where He not only speaks but also refers to Himself in the first person,

'Set apart for me Barnabas and Saul for the work to which *I* have called them' (my italics). The Holy Spirit is therefore revealed to possess all the qualities of personhood. The Bible speaks of the 'fellowship of the Holy Spirit'. We cannot have a relationship with an influence, but as a Person, the Holy Spirit is able to be our friend, companion, confidant and guide.

The Bible also states that the Holy Spirit is part of the Godhead, with the very same attributes as God the Father. In Genesis 1:2 and Job 33:4 we see He has the power to create. Psalm 139:7 declares His omnipresence and Hebrews 9:14 shows Him to be eternal. In 2 Corinthians 3:17–18 He is referred to as 'Lord' and Acts 5:1–4 shows that lying to the Holy Spirit is lying to God. Indeed His very title, *Holy* Spirit proclaims His divinity. Although we must not cast the members of the Trinity in pre-determined moulds, it can be helpful to see that each one has an individual ministry in the world. Each member of the Godhead has all the qualities and attributes of the others, but there flows through each individual member a specific ministry. We could say that the Father is *Love* (1 John 3:1), the Son is *Light* (John 1:9) and the Spirit is *Life* (Rom. 8:2).

Discussion Starters

1. Why do we believe the Holy Spirit is a Person and not merely an influence?

   _____

   _____

   _____

   _____

   _____

2. What are the attributes of the Holy Spirit's personality?

   _____

   _____

   _____

   _____

   _____

3. How do you think of the Holy Spirit?

   _____

   _____

   _____

   _____

   _____

4. Why do we believe that the Holy Spirit is God?

   _____

   _____

   _____

   _____

   _____

5. How might we hurt the Holy Spirit?

   _____

   _____

   _____

   _____

   _____

6. How might we please the Holy Spirit?

_____
_____
_____
_____
_____

7. What did Jesus reveal about the Person of the Holy Spirit?

_____
_____
_____
_____
_____

8. Why is the Holy Spirit often in the background?

_____
_____
_____
_____
_____

9. Describe what is meant by the phrase, 'fellowship of the Holy Spirit'?

_____
_____
_____
_____
_____

10. How could the Church teach more effectively about the Holy Spirit?

_____
_____
_____
_____
_____

Personal Application

Our beliefs determine our attitudes and actions. If our beliefs about the Person of the Holy Spirit are not in accordance with Scripture then we will not live in accordance with Scripture. We therefore need to honestly compare the revelation of Scripture with our own beliefs and behaviour in respect to the Holy Spirit and ask God to help us make any necessary adjustments. If we have ignored, disobeyed or grieved the Holy Spirit we may also need to ask for forgiveness. When we align our beliefs with Scripture the Spirit will be Lord and we will come to experience freedom and transformation into the Lord's likeness (2 Cor. 3:17–18). It is not primarily a matter of receiving supernatural power but of enjoying a divine companionship – the fellowship of the Holy Spirit.

Seeing Jesus in the Scriptures

Jesus was entirely dependent on the Holy Spirit for His life and ministry. He was conceived by the Holy Spirit (Luke 1:35), filled with the Holy Spirit (Luke 3:22), He ministered in the power of the Spirit (Luke 4:14) and even offered Himself for our sins through the eternal Spirit (Heb. 9:14). If the sinless Son of God was so reliant on the Holy Spirit to fulfil God's will for His life, how much more do we need to understand and depend on the Spirit in our own lives.

WEEK 2

The Holy Spirit in the Old Testament

Opening Icebreaker

Ask the group to recall key points from the last session and how much they can remember about the Holy Spirit in the Old Testament.

Bible Readings

- Genesis 1:1–5
- Exodus 35:30–34
- Numbers 11:16–29
- Deuteronomy 34:9
- Judges 13:24–25; 15:14–15
- 1 Samuel 16:13

Opening Our Eyes

The very first inspired picture of the Holy Spirit we have in the Bible is found in the opening verses of the book of Genesis. The earth is without form and void but in the heart of the Spirit there exists an intense longing to bring order out of the chaos. The word 'hovering' in verse 2 gives the picture of a Being of intense emotion brooding over a chaotic universe and seized with an intense desire to bring harmony and beauty into the scene. Our first introduction to the Holy Spirit shows Him to be a Person of deep compassion and concern. He not only played a major part in the creation of the universe but also in the creation of men and women (Gen. 2:7; Job 33:4). The Holy Spirit is often revealed in the Old Testament through symbols such as: a dove, breath, oil and wind. These are the subject of more detailed study in Week 4 but there are a number of other passages which explain the Person and ministry of the Spirit prior to the birth of Jesus.

In many ways the operation of the Holy Spirit in the Old Testament is quite different from His activity in the midst of the present-day Church. Due to the fact that sin had struck deep into the heart of the human race, He was obliged to move upon *selected people* on *specific occasions* and for *special purposes*. We see this clearly in the story of Samson when several times we read, 'the Spirit of the LORD came upon him in power'. The book of Judges contains other examples of this phenomenon and includes Othniel who became Israel's leader and led them into battle, resulting in 40 years of peace (Judg. 3:9–11). Similarly, the Spirit of the Lord came upon Gideon (Judg. 6:34) and Jephthah (Judg. 11:29) to deliver God's people from oppression. This anointing for leadership was relatively common and can be found in the story of the 70 elders (Num. 11:16–26) as well as that of individuals such as Saul and David (1 Sam. 10:6; 16:13). An interesting aspect of the Spirit's work was that in a number of cases the recipients did not seem to be aware of His presence. Samson, for example, after his encounter with Delilah, tried to fight as before 'but he did not know that the LORD had left him' (Judg. 16:20). Also, Moses after being with God on Mount Sinai, 'was not aware that his face was radiant' with the glory of the Lord (Exod. 34:29).

The Holy Spirit not only came upon people in power but also to guide and impart special wisdom and skill. In Exodus we discover that Bezalel was filled 'with the Spirit of God, with skill, ability and knowledge in all kinds of crafts' as he led the team constructing the tabernacle – the movable tent where people worshipped in the wilderness. God also gave both Bezalel and Oholiab a special ability to teach others their skills.

On numerous occasions the Holy Spirit came upon people to speak messages from God and prophesy. In 2 Samuel 23:2 David states, 'The Spirit of the LORD spoke through me; his word was on my tongue.' We also see the Spirit operating in this way in the lives of people such as Azariah (2 Chron. 15:1–8), Jahaziel (2 Chron. 20:14) and even the ungodly Balaam (Num. 24:1–3).

Discussion Starters

1. How is the Holy Spirit revealed in the Old Testament?

_____

_____

_____

_____

2. For what purpose did the Holy Spirit come upon people in the Old Testament?

_____

_____

_____

_____

3. List the different ministries of the Holy Spirit in the Old Testament.

_____

_____

_____

_____

4. Why would the Holy Spirit come upon the ungodly Balaam?

_____

_____

_____

_____

5. Why did the Spirit depart from Saul?

_____

_____

_____

_____

6. Why did the Spirit depart from Samson?

_____
_____
_____
_____

7. Why were people not aware of the Spirit upon them?

_____
_____
_____
_____

8. Do you think the Spirit enhances our abilities or gives us new ones?

_____
_____
_____
_____

9. Why did the Spirit come upon Eldad and Medad and how did Joshua and Moses react?

_____
_____
_____
_____

10. How was the Spirit imparted to people and is this still appropriate today?

_____
_____
_____
_____

Personal Application

The Spirit hovered over a darkened and chaotic universe in indescribable anguish and concern. We can sometimes find ourselves in situations that are so confusing it seems like darkness and despair has descended on our spiritual experience. Although unrecognized and unfelt, the Holy Spirit hovers over the chaos and confusion of our lives to bring order and light at just the right moment through a creative miracle. Remember, God's Word speaks light into the darkness, the Spirit is there with you, communicating the warmth of His love and the deep concern of His heart. It is often not the situation that brings despair but the sense of hopelessness that accompanies it. But we are a people who believe in a God of hope and know that the same heavenly Dove that brought breathtaking beauty to a forlorn and empty world can work a similar miracle in our own lives.

Seeing Jesus in the Scriptures

In the Old Testament we read that the Spirit would come upon people for a special purpose and then, because of their sin or the accomplishment of the divine assignment, He would depart. Not so with Jesus, who received the 'spirit without limit' for eternity (John 3:34; Acts 2:33).

WEEK 3

The Work of the Holy Spirit

Opening Icebreaker

Ask people to share the key points of how the Holy Spirit worked in the Old Testament.

Bible Readings

- John 3:1–8; 14:26; 16:7–15
- Romans 8:26–27
- 1 Corinthians 2:6–16; 3:16
- 2 Corinthians 3:3, 16–18

Opening Our Eyes

Although we see the Holy Spirit at work in the Old Testament, His ministry is only fully revealed in the New Testament. One of the main roles of the Holy Spirit is to *glorify Jesus*. Once when I was in India I saw an evening marriage procession where friends of the bridegroom walked alongside him and shone torches illuminating his face for all to see. The work of the Holy Spirit is like that, He comes to light up the face of Jesus and focus our attention on our Saviour. We, the Church, His bride, can look forward with anticipation to our marriage with the Lamb (Rev. 19:6–9).

In John 16:8, the Holy Spirit *convicts* or *convinces* us of three things, 'guilt in regard to sin and [the need of] righteousness and [God's] judgment'. Note that it is guilt of falling below God's standards not unnecessary false guilt of failing our own standards that can cripple the personality. We may witness to someone for years but it is only the Holy Spirit that genuinely convicts a person of their own sinfulness before a holy God. The Holy Spirit also assures or convinces us that we are loved by God, saved by His grace and embraced as His children (Rom. 8:14–16).

We come into the kingdom of God through the birth of the Holy Spirit or not at all. Dr E.S. Jones said, 'The birth of the Spirit is that change, gradual or sudden, by which we who are children of the first birth, through a physical birth into a physical world, become children of the second birth through a *spiritual birth* into a spiritual world' (my emphasis). Being born into a Christian home or attending church does not make us Christians any more than being born in a garage or going to a petrol station makes us a car.

No one can truly understand the Person of God and the real meaning of the Scriptures without the *revelation* of the Holy Spirit. For a person to understand God and His Word by human intellect alone is just as impossible as it is for an unsighted person to judge a beauty contest! Of course one can know the language, history, geography and literature of the Bible but its real meaning remains a mystery without the Holy Spirit. He is the One who reveals God the Father to us, glorifies Jesus and helps us not just to know Scripture but to understand it and experience its truths. The Holy Spirit does not simply reveal truth to our minds, but guides us to apply it to our lives. He takes us by the hand and seeks to turn the ideal into the real, aspiration into acceptance and makes everything operate in the here and now.

The Holy Spirit *transforms us* to be more like Jesus. I can remember my pastor telling me when I was a teenager, 'The Holy Spirit will make you Christlike.' I felt rather threatened by that statement because I didn't want anything that would curb my personality. However, I came to see that Christlikeness, far from curbing the personality, completes it, because attributes such as love, faithfulness and forgiveness help maximise our potential.

One of His roles is to be a *personal Companion, Comforter, Guide* and *Friend*. The Holy Spirit *helps* us when we feel weak and gives us strength, wisdom and courage for the path ahead.

Discussion Starters

1. How does the Holy Spirit glorify Jesus?

_____

_____

_____

_____

_____

2. What is the difference between human guilt and spiritual conviction?

_____

_____

_____

_____

_____

3. Why do we need a second birth?

_____

_____

_____

_____

_____

4. Describe your own story of becoming a Christian.

_____

_____

_____

_____

_____

5. How does the Holy Spirit reveal the real meaning of the Scriptures to us?

_____

_____

_____

_____

6. Compare human knowledge and spiritual revelation.

_____
_____
_____
_____
_____

7. How does the Holy Spirit make us more Christlike?

_____
_____
_____
_____
_____

8. How does the Holy Spirit help us?

_____
_____
_____
_____
_____

9. Contrast and compare the work of the Holy Spirit in the Old and New Testaments.

_____
_____
_____
_____
_____

Personal Application

The purpose of this session is not that we might academically know how the Holy Spirit works, but that we might experience the Holy Spirit working in and through us! Information should result in transformation and knowing Bible references into knowing personal revelation. Our beliefs must become our experiences else our faith is destined for a museum or mausoleum.

If we would learn wisdom from a friend we would have to give them an opportunity to speak to us in private and ensure that we ourselves have stopped talking and have tuned in to their voice. So it is with the Holy Spirit. He is a gentleman who will not force His way into our lives but will immediately respond to our invitation as we quietly wait for Him. Trying to work for Christ without the Holy Spirit is like pushing a car along the road – all effort and no power. Instead, turn on the engine, sit back and experience the ride of your life!

Seeing Jesus in the Scriptures

We see a remarkable change in the ministry of the Holy Spirit through the life of Christ. Whereas before Christ, the Spirit had come upon people in measure for a season, now He was given to Jesus 'without limit'. This was a precursor to the time after Jesus was glorified, when on the Day of Pentecost He poured out the Spirit on all people (Acts 2:17, 33).

WEEK 4

Symbols of the Holy Spirit

Opening Icebreaker

What symbols are used to depict countries such as Canada, the USA, England and Wales? Can you think of other countries or organisations which use symbols, eg, the Olympics? What do these symbols indicate?

Bible Readings

- 1 Samuel 16:1–13
- Matthew 3:1–17
- John 3:1–8; 7:37–39

Opening Our Eyes

The Bible is full of symbolic language and illustrations.
It may be said that God Himself invented visual aids!
A symbol is a representation of something that conveys
an element of information or truth. This is especially
so of the Holy Spirit who is often likened to familiar items
so that we can learn more of His nature and ministry.

A *dove* is universally acknowledged as a symbol of peace.
Why? Undoubtedly it is based on the story of Noah's ark.
Two birds went out from the ark – a raven and a dove.
Being an unclean bird, the raven did not return (Lev.
11:15). It would have alighted on the floating carcasses
of the dead and eaten the rotting flesh. At first the dove
returned because the corruption of the earth was
offensive. Later it returned with an olive leaf and then
finally left the ark altogether. The season of judgment had
passed, leaving peace on earth. What a beautiful picture
this is of the descent of the Spirit on our Lord Jesus Christ
during His baptism in the River Jordan. The Holy Spirit
went to and fro looking for someone on whom He could
remain but there was no one worthy. He did come upon
men and women temporarily but it was only when He
came upon Christ that He remained.

Oil is another powerful symbol of the Holy Spirit. In
1 Samuel 16:13 we read, 'Samuel took the horn of oil and
anointed him in the presence of his brothers, and from
that day on the Spirit of the LORD came upon David in
power' (my italics). The ancient tabernacle and all its
furniture and utensils were anointed with oil to
consecrate them and make them *holy*. Dedication and
consecration are not complete unless they lead to
ministration, so Aaron and his sons were anointed to
serve the Lord (Exod. 30:22–33; Lev. 8:1–12). In 1 Samuel
9:16 is recorded God's instruction to Samuel regarding
Saul, 'Anoint him leader … he will deliver

my people from the hand of the Philistines.' We might call this being anointed to *save*.

Jesus Himself used *water* as a symbol of the Holy Spirit. In Genesis 21:14–19 the water in Hagar's bottle was soon exhausted, but the Lord opened her eyes and she saw an everlasting well of water. When our natural resources are exhausted, the Holy Spirit gives us new vision and revives us again and again. Water cleanses, refreshes, sustains life and causes barren desert to blossom with beauty and fruitfulness (Ezek. 47:1–12; Rev. 22:1–2). What a wonderful symbol for the Holy Spirit and His work in our lives!

To come into contact with the Holy Spirit is to come into contact with *fire*. A coal from the altar purified Isaiah's lips, removed his guilt and atoned for his sins (Isa. 6:1–11).

On the Day of Pentecost the Holy Spirit came with the sound like 'the blowing of a violent *wind*' (Acts 2:2, my italics). Wind cannot be seen but it can most certainly be felt. It is the invisible but powerful operation of the Holy Spirit by which we are born again into the kingdom of God. It was the *breath* of wind in Ezekiel 37 that caused the dry bones to come together and live as a mighty army. The wind carries with it scents and how wonderful that the wind of the Holy Spirit brings to us the fragrance of Jesus and blows over our souls to carry that fragrance to others.

Discussion Starters

1. How helpful do you find the use of symbols to convey spiritual truth?

   _____
   _____
   _____
   _____

2. Why did the dove return to the ark but the raven kept flying back and forth?

   _____
   _____
   _____
   _____
   _____

3. Why is the Holy Spirit likened to fire?

   _____
   _____
   _____
   _____

4. Why is the Holy Spirit likened to water?

   _____
   _____
   _____
   _____

5. Why is the Holy Spirit likened to wind?

   _____
   _____
   _____
   _____

6. How does the Old Testament anointing of oil apply to a Christian today?

_____
_____
_____
_____

7. Which symbol of the Holy Spirit have you most experienced?

_____
_____
_____
_____

8. Which symbol of the Holy Spirit have you least experienced?

_____
_____
_____
_____

9. How have trials and difficulties served to strengthen your faith?

_____
_____
_____
_____

10. Can you identify any other symbols of the Holy Spirit?

_____
_____
_____
_____

Personal Application

Jesus instructed us to be as 'innocent as doves' (Matt. 10:16). As we pursue holiness and purity in our lives so the Holy Spirit will alight on us, remain with us and reveal more of God to us (Matt. 5:8; Heb. 12:14).

Just as in the book of Leviticus the anointing oil made everything that it touched holy, so believers receive God's holiness when they encounter the Spirit. We have no inherent holiness, but John writing to Christians in the first century said, 'you have an anointing from the Holy One' (1 John 2:20). We are made holy as the Holy Spirit anoints us. The Spirit's specific ministry is to bring the resources of the Godhead to us, to deposit them in our lives and produce in us the same kind of holiness that characterised the life of Christ.

How we also need to drink from the well of the Holy Spirit. The water bottle of church activities and past experiences will inevitably be exhausted, but the well of the Holy Spirit never runs dry and will ensure we are always spiritually fresh.

Seeing Jesus in the Scriptures

Jesus is gentle like a dove (Matt. 11:28–30), He was anointed by the Holy Spirit, He gives us the water of life and breathes the Spirit on us as He did the first disciples (John 20:22).

WEEK 5

The Fruit of the Holy Spirit

Opening Icebreaker

Cut up different fruits into small pieces and then ask some blindfolded volunteers to taste and try to identify them. It will be more interesting if you use some unusual fruits such as passion fruit, kiwi and tomato. Ask people to write a list of as many fruits as they can. What are people's favourites and why?

Bible Readings

- John 15:1–17
- 2 Corinthians 6:3–10
- Galatians 5:22–24
- Ephesians 5:8–10
- Colossians 3:12–14
- 2 Peter 1:3–8

29

Opening Our Eyes

The nine qualities which go to make up Christian character are the natural outcome of the Holy Spirit's indwelling of the believer. Paul speaks of the *fruit* of the Spirit, which suggests something that is effortless.

The Greek language has four words for *love*: *eros* meaning sexual love, *philia* which is affectionate human love, *storge* which refers to family love and *agape,* which is God's unconditional love exemplified in Jesus and His sacrifice. Paul says the 'the love of Christ controls us' (2 Cor. 5:14, RSV). It is possible for us to be controlled by the love of success, money or a cause. What controls you – the love of a cause or the love of Christ? Don't try to manufacture love – linger in the shadow of the cross, the love of God finds its most burning expression there.

It is no accident that *joy* follows love for it is its by-product. We cannot deny that there is a good deal of suffering in Christianity, but at the heart of our faith is an Easter morning of resurrection and the forgiveness of sins. That means there is always good reason to rejoice. We must distinguish between supernatural joy and mere happiness. Happiness depends on what happens and is linked to our health and wealth. Christian joy is independent of circumstances and bursts forth even in pain, persecution and prison (Acts 16:22–25).

In classical Greek, the word for *peace* was mainly negative, implying freedom from war, but in the New Testament the word embodies the Hebrew concept of 'shalom' emphasising serenity and harmony. Peace is not passivity, mental gymnastics, withdrawal or resignation. It is a quality of mind and spirit which experiences contentment and confidence in knowing and trusting God regardless of outward circumstances.

The fourth fruit is an attitude to people which never loses *patience* with them, however unreasonable they may be, and never loses hope for them, however unlovely and unteachable they may be. That is why another translation is long-suffering. *Kindness* is not indulgence, sentimentality or lack of firmness, but treating others the way God has treated us. He freely gives rain on the just and unjust (Matt. 5:45). *Goodness* is primarily an attitude that thinks of others first, not merely performing a series of 'good turns' for them.

Faithfulness is not the depth of our belief but the quality of reliability or trustworthiness which makes a person someone on whom we can utterly rely and on whose word we can totally depend.

The Greek word *prautes* is translated gentleness but I prefer *humility* or *meekness*. The person in whom the Spirit dwells is meek and humble – just like Christ who was 'meek and lowly in heart' (Matt. 11:29, AV). Ancient writers regarded humility as a 'servile, grovelling spirit'. However, this quality is not self-belittlement but a spirit of lowliness that sees no embarrassment in washing people's feet and a spirit of obedience to authority that displays no rebellion, arrogance or independence. Insecure people dare not be humble, but the humble are great in the kingdom of God.

Self-control is not the self being in control but the Holy Spirit giving us the ability to control ourselves. This is not a matter of the will but the result of the Holy Spirit so motivating our lives that we are no longer controlled by our passions for things such as food, sex, ambition, possessions or revenge resulting in wasted empty lives. Instead our lives are purposeful and fruitful and we realise the full potential of our God-given talents.

Discussion Starters

1. Why is Christian love greater than any other type
of love? How does the description of love in
1 Corinthians 13 embrace other spiritual fruit?

_____
_____
_____
_____

2. Define meekness. Why is meekness not a weakness?

_____
_____
_____
_____

3. How could Moses lead a nation and order executions
yet be described as 'more humble than anyone else
on the face of the earth'? (Num. 12:3)

_____
_____
_____
_____

4. Why is the supernatural peace of Christ different
to the world's definition of peace?

_____
_____
_____
_____

5. To what extent is your own happiness based
on circumstances?

_____
_____
_____
_____

6. How might God prune us so that we become more
fruitful?

_____

_____

_____

_____

7. How does goodness differ from kindness?

_____

_____

_____

_____

8. What might limit our ability to produce spiritual fruit?

_____

_____

_____

_____

9. If a plant needs water, sunlight and good soil to
be fruitful, what do Christians need to be spiritually
fruitful?

_____

_____

_____

_____

10. What fruit are you most lacking in your life and
how could you develop them? You could pray for
each other.

_____

_____

_____

_____

Personal Application

The Christian in whom the fruit of the Spirit is fully
evident is the best portrait of Christianity and witness
of the faith. How would God paint such a Christian? His
brushes are the Scriptures. The colours on His palette
are love, joy, peace, patience, kindness, goodness,
faithfulness, humility and self-control. The absence of
any one of these is serious, just as a rainbow does not
appear as a true rainbow if one of its colours is missing.
The model God uses is His own dear Son, in whom
every characteristic is seen to its utmost perfection and
wondrously balanced by every other. Even now, God's
brush strokes are at work, gently and lovingly caressing
into your nature all the lineaments of our Lord's character.
All He asks is that you hold still – stop trying and start
trusting and allow Him to complete His work so that by
your love and fruit all people might know that you are
His disciple. Are you plagued by bad temper when
people are unreasonable or fail to keep their promises?
Seek God for the fruit of patience. Are you anxious about
the future? Seek God for the fruit of peace.

Meditate on His love, for when you realise how much
God loves you an amazing effect is produced in you –
you begin to love like Him.

Seeing Jesus in the Scriptures

Jesus is our example of a truly fruit-filled life. His agape
sacrificial love led to His crucifixion for our sins. Jesus
was a Person of immense joy and He possessed a sense
of peace that the world had never seen before.

WEEK 6

The Gifts of the Holy Spirit

Opening Icebreaker

What memorable gifts have you received for your birthday, Christmas etc and what made them special? What distinguishes a gift from a reward?

Bible Readings

- Romans 12:1–8
- 1 Corinthians 12:1–31; 14:1–5, 39–40

Opening Our Eyes

Not so many years ago, the majority of Christians believed that gifts were not for today, but most now accept that the Holy Spirit is still bestowing special abilities on members of Christ's Body. All gifts are to enable the Church to function efficiently and effectively in the world, and they are not to be used as ego-building devices. We must be clear in the *supernatural* character of these endowments. The nine gifts listed in 1 Corinthians 12:7–10 are not the result of educational ability, natural prowess or human learning, but are entirely supernatural in their scope, structure and administration. They cannot be purchased, earned or merited and may be given irrespective of personal charm or temperament.

Paul specifically wrote to the Corinthian disciples that he did not want them to be ignorant about spiritual gifts. He described nine separate gifts which can easily be divided into three natural groupings: 1. *Gifts of Inspiration* – tongues, interpretation and prophecy. 2. *Gifts of Demonstration* – faith, healing and miracles. 3. *Gifts of Revelation* – word of knowledge, word of wisdom and discerning of spirits. We might refer to these groups as gifts of speaking, gifts of doing and gifts of knowing.

The *gift of tongues* is a supernatural ability to speak in an unlearned human or angelic language (1 Cor. 13:1). It can be used privately to strengthen our faith (14:4a) but must always be accompanied by the *gift of interpretation* if used publicly (14:28). The *gift of prophecy* does not primarily refer to predicting the future, but is an ability to speak a special message from God to strengthen, encourage and comfort (1 Cor. 14:3).

The *gift of faith* is a supernatural confidence in God for a naturally impossible situation. Although sometimes abused, the *gift of healing* others in the power of the

Spirit has been part of church life for two millennia. The *gift of miracles* is releasing the creative power of God into human life and circumstances.

The *word of knowledge* is not a gift of *all* knowledge but operates when the Holy Spirit imparts a fragment of His knowledge for a temporary and specific purpose. Similarly there is a *word of wisdom* which is a flash of divine insight that illuminates the path ahead when situations are especially dark and confusing. The *discerning of spirits* operates so the believer can understand the spiritual source of a particular issue or problem.

We must not limit the operation of the Spirit to only these nine gifts, however, for 1 Corinthians 12:28 refers to 'gifts of administration' and we have already seen that Bezalel was filled 'with the Spirit of God, with skill, ability and knowledge in all kinds of crafts' (Exod. 31:2). The list of gifts in Romans 12 includes preaching, serving, teaching, encouraging, empathising and giving.

Some Christians try to avoid anything to do with the supernatural but if we erased the supernatural from the book of the Acts of the Early Church we would have very little left! There would be no tongues of fire, no lame man leaping for joy, no opening of prison doors and no world shaken by the power of the gospel! Listen to what Jesus said before He returned to His Father in heaven, '… anyone who has faith in me will do what I have been doing. He will do even greater things than these …' (John 14:12).

Discussion Starters

1. What is the purpose of the gifts of the Holy Spirit?

_____

_____

_____

_____

2. Who decides who has which gift?

_____

_____

_____

_____

3. How relevant are the gifts in the modern Church?

_____

_____

_____

_____

4. Why is the gift of tongues different?

_____

_____

_____

_____

5. Which gifts have you seen in operation?

_____

_____

_____

_____

6. Does anything about the gifts of the Spirit cause you concern?

_____
_____
_____
_____
_____

7. Why might some gifts of the Spirit be related to our natural talents or learned abilities?

_____
_____
_____
_____
_____

8. What active role might we play in obtaining or developing gifts of the Spirit?

_____
_____
_____
_____
_____

9. What gifts and abilities do you see in other members of your group? How can they best be expressed/used in and by the group?

_____
_____
_____
_____
_____

Personal Application

Although gifts are given, not earned, we are encouraged to desire and seek the gifts of the Holy Spirit. This is a paradox but is consistent within Scripture. God's blessings are freely given, yet 'the eyes of the LORD range throughout the earth to strengthen those whose hearts are fully committed to him' (2 Chron. 16:9), and 'You do not have, because you do not ask God' (James 4:2). We are exhorted to 'eagerly desire the greater gifts' and 'spiritual gifts ...' (1 Cor. 12:31; 14:1). This is not a suggestion but an instruction that if followed will bring a sense of fulfilment to our own lives, strength to the church in which we worship and blessing to the lives of those with whom we come into contact. The story of Stephen and the appointment of deacons is a fascinating insight into the inter-relationship of the natural and the supernatural. Stephen was simply appointed for practical service in the daily distribution of food but he did 'great wonders and miraculous signs among the people' (Acts 6:8). The Holy Spirit longs to manifest His presence and power through our everyday practical tasks.

Seeing Jesus in the Scriptures

Jesus relied totally on the revelation and power of God rather than any of His own abilities. He said, 'I tell you the truth, the Son can do nothing by himself; he can do only what he sees his Father doing' (John 5:19). If Jesus needed the power of God in His life then we also must need the Holy Spirit in order to fulfil God's purposes for our own lives.

WEEK 7

The Spirit-Filled Life

Opening Icebreaker

Ask everyone to share (briefly!) what has particularly impacted them from the previous studies and how their own understanding or appreciation of the Holy Spirit has changed over the last few weeks

Bible Readings

- Luke 11:11–13
- Acts 2:1–4; 4:23–31
- Galatians 5:16–18
- Ephesians 5:15–21
- 1 Thessalonians 5:19

Opening Our Eyes

The Day of Pentecost marked a dramatic change in the operation of the Holy Spirit. On that day disciples who had previously been in a locked room for fear of the Jews were transformed into people ablaze with the Spirit who turned the world upside down (John 20:19; Acts 17:6, NKJV)! Although we may hold different theological views of the filling of the Spirit, all Christians agree on one thing – we need day by day to allow the Spirit to enter fully into every part of our being, remove all blockages and transform us into perpetual channels of blessing.

The text of Ephesians 5:18 in the Amplified Bible reads thus: 'And do not get drunk with wine … but ever be filled and stimulated with the Holy Spirit.' This is not a one-off event like conversion but a continual every day occurrence. Many commentators have pointed out that this verse is not a promise to be experienced but a command to be obeyed. However we view the doctrine of the Holy Spirit or whatever experience we may have had of Him in the past, if we do not have a continuous and ever-present flow of His power and presence in our lives then we are living below the level God intends. Someone heard Billy Graham pray to be filled with the Spirit and said to him, 'I thought you had been filled.' 'I have,' replied Billy, 'but the trouble is I leak.'

We have already seen how the Holy Spirit *clothes* us with power and *contributes* to our fruitfulness. He also acts as our *comforter*. The special word Jesus used in John 14:16 to describe the Holy Spirit, *Paraclete*, is made up of two Greek words, *para* (alongside) and *kaleo* (call) – one who is called alongside to help. In many modern Bibles it is translated 'Counsellor' but older versions use the word 'Comforter'. Being filled with the Spirit is not just about visible fruit and gifts but He is also there to minister to our hurts and bind our wounds. I meet scores of people who carry within them past feelings of rejection. These unhealed hurts put a weight on their personality that can be too heavy to bear and the person, as we say, 'breaks down'. The Holy Spirit, if we let Him, can fill us and heal the hurts of rejection, disappointment, failure, false accusation and even deep trauma. Joni Eareckson Tada was a beautiful vivacious teenager when she was paralysed by a diving accident and is now a quadraplegic. At first she was angry and bitter, but the Holy Spirit has so comforted her that she has painted award-winning pictures with a brush held between her teeth, authored a number of inspiring books and travels the world encouraging others with her faith in God.

Jesus used three prepositions to describe how the Holy Spirit touches our lives. In John 14:17 He said, '... he lives *with* you and will be *in* you' (my italics). In Acts 1:8 Jesus also explained what would happen when 'the Holy Spirit has come *upon* you' (NKJV, my italics). The Holy Spirit who is *with* us to guide, teach and convict us of sin would be *in* us to convert and regenerate; He would also come *upon* us to clothe us with supernatural power and abilities so we can manifest the resurrection life of Christ to the world.

Discussion Starters

1. What happened at Pentecost?

_____

_____

_____

_____

2. What are the qualities of a Spirit-filled life?

_____

_____

_____

_____

3. How do the Greek words used by Jesus help us understand the role of the Holy Spirit?

_____

_____

_____

_____

4. How do the different prepositions used by Jesus help us understand the function of the Holy Spirit in our lives?

_____

_____

_____

_____

5. Why do we need to be filled with the Holy Spirit?

_____

_____

_____

_____

6. Why does being filled with the Spirit differ from conversion?

_____

_____

_____

_____

7. How could you develop your relationship with the Holy Spirit?

_____

_____

_____

_____

8. How might we 'put out the Spirit's fire'?

_____

_____

_____

_____

9. How exactly do we 'live by the Spirit'?

_____

_____

_____

_____

10. Do you feel any anxiety about being filled with the Spirit?

_____

_____

_____

_____

Personal Application

Let's now focus on the steps you need to take in order to experience for yourself more of the power and presence of the Holy Spirit.

1. Examine yourself to see how much you lack in your own abilities and need the Holy Spirit in your life.

2. Is there any unresolved conflict, unrepented sin or personal issue you must put right (Acts 8:18–24)?

3. Remind yourself God is more willing to give the Holy Spirit than you are to receive (Luke 11:11–13).

4. Make receiving the Holy Spirit a priority in your life (eg being full of the Spirit has a greater demand on your time and ambitions than hobbies or leisure).

5. Match God's self-giving with your own giving of self totally to Him.

6. Ask for the Holy Spirit and reach out in faith to receive Him.

7. Set your life to obey the Holy Spirit.

Seeing Jesus in the Scriptures

It was after Jesus demonstrated obedience to His Father by being baptised, despite John's hesitation, that the Spirit came upon Him in the form of a dove. Only then did He begin His public ministry and people were touched by the power of God flowing through Him (Matt. 3:12–17; Luke 3:21–23). We also need to be obedient to God in order to receive and be filled with the Spirit. We do not need to be perfect, but we do need to be willing and seek after God.

Leader's Notes

Week 1: The Person of the Holy Spirit

Opening Icebreaker

If we identify the basic characteristics of personality such as individuality, self-awareness, the ability to think, feel and decide, then we see that the Holy Spirit is not merely an influence but is actually a Person.

Bible Readings

Although a number of references are given to read, it would also be helpful to read extra verses quoted in the notes where time permits.

Aim of the Session

Many people, including a number of Christians, think of the Holy Spirit as an 'it'. When we deny that the Holy Spirit is a Person, even unconsciously, we weaken the very faith we proclaim. Some Christians believe He is an impersonal influence even while using personal pronouns such as 'He' and 'His' when referring to Him. I remember on one occasion pointing out the illogicality of this to someone who held this view, and this was his reply, 'I use a personal pronoun when talking about the Holy Spirit in the same way that people use the term "Jack Frost" when speaking about icy conditions.' What nonsense! We may use personal pronouns for inanimate objects like ships (she), but this is not the way the divinely-inspired Scriptures speak of the Holy Spirit. Jesus Himself spoke of the Holy Spirit as a Person referring to 'Him' and 'He'.

The aim of this, our first session, is to expose wrong perceptions of the Holy Spirit and lay the foundation for the rest of our studies. Not only is the Holy Spirit clearly referred to in Scripture as a Person, He is also proclaimed in no uncertain terms to be part of the Godhead. People who acknowledge Him as a Person can sometimes fail to grasp this vital truth. They accept His personhood but deny His divinity. Somehow the Holy Spirit is seen as less than God. Although certainly less prominent in the Scriptures than the Father or the Son, the Holy Spirit is shown very clearly to be divine. The Holy Spirit, like the Son, is obedient to the Father but nonetheless possesses all the qualities of divinity. In this respect it is important not to argue the point from human reasoning but by reading the relevant scriptures quoted in the section Opening Our Eyes, where He is revealed to be holy, omnipresent and eternal. It is not a matter of debate but of accepting the truth of the divine revelation already recorded in God's Word.

What evidence do we have in the Scriptures for the Spirit's specific ministry being that of life? The Holy Spirit has functioned in the two greatest creative acts of life – the old creation of the physical universe and the new creation of our salvation. It is interesting to note that when God breathed life into man in Genesis 2:7, it was the energy of the Holy Spirit that produced life. 'The Spirit of God has made me; the breath of the Almighty gives me life' (Job 33:4). Similarly, the book of Romans records: 'And if the Spirit of him who raised Jesus from the dead is living in you, he who raised Christ from the dead will also give life to your mortal bodies through his Spirit, who lives in you' (8:11).

Week 2: The Holy Spirit in the Old Testament

Opening Icebreaker

The main points from the last session to reinforce are
that the Holy Spirit is a Person and that He is a member
of the Godhead. It will be interesting to discover what
most people in the group already understand about the
Holy Spirit in the Old Testament. You can then adapt the
material for the session accordingly.

Bible Readings

The readings encompass different examples of the Holy
Spirit in the Old Testament and additional references are
given in the text. In order to answer the Discussion Starter
about the Spirit departing from Saul and Samson you may
also need to refer to Judges 16 and 1 Samuel 15 and 16:14.

Aim of the Session

The aim is to show that the Holy Spirit plays an important
part in the story of the Old Testament. (He is more
usually referred to as the Spirit of the Lord or the Spirit
of God in the Old Testament.) Although He is often in the
background His role is vital in creation, in empowering
Israel's leaders and equipping people for service. A
careful study of the operation of the Holy Spirit in the
lives of Old Testament characters leads us to the
conclusion that the Spirit came upon men and women
to fulfil a temporary purpose, and then departed when
the mission was accomplished.

Despite the signs, wonders and miracles, we see the way
in which He often used people whose lives lacked the
quality of holiness and righteousness. Some Christians
have wondered why God should have used such people
when their lives denied one of the most important aspects
of the Godhead. We might puzzle why the Holy Spirit
would come upon the disobedient Saul, adulterous

Samson and murderous David. The answer is quite simple – God used the imperfect as a point in a line leading toward the *progressive revelation* that a day would come when He would not only impart His power but also His purity. It was only with the coming of the Lord Jesus Christ that the Spirit could be given without measure. Although God appears to use people in the Old Testament whose lives lacked holiness, it is not because He approves of their sin. This is emphasised by the withdrawal of the Spirit from Saul and Samson, and also by the way God sent Nathan to confront David of his sin (2 Sam. 12:1–14). In the historical books the Spirit of God is seen in relation to some *unusual and extraordinary activity* of God in the life of an individual when there is a definite step forward in the plans and purposes of God. For example, God wants to deliver His people from slavery or oppression and will temporarily use anyone who will obey Him. Ultimately the sinful acts of some God had chosen and anointed led to the removal of the Holy Spirit from their lives.

It is clear that the Spirit's work in the lives of some people in the Old Testament was in a sense superficial because He did not penetrate the inner depth of their beings and bring a deep change in their characters to produce qualities of godliness. However, the prophet Joel promises that a new day will come when the Spirit will no longer be given occasionally and specially but constantly and perpetually (Joel 2:28–29). Ezekiel, too, looks forward to the time when the Holy Spirit would come with an impartation of power, not simply for a task, but to make people clean and keep them clean (Ezek. 11:19–20; 36:25–27).

Week 3: The Work of the Holy Spirit

Opening Icebreaker
The Holy Spirit often worked independently of people in the Old Testament. When He did work through people it was usually for a specific purpose through selected individuals on special occasions. This will contrast with the way the Holy Spirit is seen to work in the life of New Testament believers.

Bible Readings
It might be useful to produce a handout by copying the list below from the book of John as well as reading the main references given

Aim of the Session
The aim of this session is to understand more about the ministry of the Holy Spirit. We have already seen how He operated in the Old Testament, but it is only when we read the New Testament that He can be fully appreciated. In fact our Lord put His disciples through a deliberate course of training on the Person and work of the Holy Spirit. This should not surprise us, for He had chosen them to teach and train others. How and what He taught would therefore be crucial. We find this course of teaching unfolded best in John's Gospel. There are in fact 12 lessons, which can be summarised thus:

- Christ was filled with the Spirit Himself and would impart the Spirit to others – John 1:33

- We can only enter the kingdom of God by the new birth of the Spirit – John 3:1–8

- The Holy Spirit's ministry was limited in the Old Testament but is without limit through Christ – John 3:34

- The Holy Spirit longs not only to flow into believers but also to flow out through them – John 7:37–39

- The Holy Spirit would abide or remain with believers permanently instead of temporarily – John 14:16

- The Holy Spirit would teach, reveal and bring to our remembrance the things of God – John 14:26

- The Holy Spirit would cause and empower us to witness the truth of Christ to others – John 15:26–27

- The Holy Spirit would convince people of the truth of their sin and eternal judgment – John 16:8

- The Holy Spirit would guide believers into all truth – John 16:13

- The Holy Spirit would give us deeper insight of not just the past or present but also the future – John 16:13

- The Holy Spirit would focus attention on Jesus and cause Him to be glorified – John 16:14

- The Holy Spirit could be received personally as a gift – John 20:22

There are other lessons on the work of the Spirit, especially relating to fruit and gifts, which will follow in Weeks 5 and 6.

Week 4: Symbols of the Holy Spirit

Opening Icebreaker

The symbols of these countries would be a maple leaf, eagle, lion and dragon. The Olympics use five overlapping rings depicting the five continents. Symbols often portray a key element about an organisation, eg a lion indicates authority, power and bravery. Christians often use the symbol of the cross as a reminder and declaration of the crucifixion of Jesus by which we are saved from punishment for our sins and enter into relationship with God.

Bible Readings

Examples of symbols are given in the readings but it would also be useful to read some of the other references given in the section Opening Our Eyes.

Aim of the Session

The purpose of this session is to understand the extensive use in Scripture of symbolism to teach about the work and ministry of the Holy Spirit. Additional notes for some of the symbols are given below:

Doves are regarded as innocent and gentle (Matt. 10:16). In my research into the nature and habits of the dove I came across this: 'One reason for the supposed gentleness of the dove is because it has no gall; gall being considered by the naturalists of old as the source and fountain of contention, the bitterness of the gall being supposed to infuse itself into the spirit.' Of one thing we can be sure – there is no bitterness in the Holy Spirit, only gentleness.

It is interesting to note the three prohibitions in relation to the anointing oil. First, it was to be put on the clothes and not the flesh. Second, it was only to be put on a priest and third, no imitation of it was to be made. The command not to put oil on the flesh suggests that God wants the spiritual to have absolute sway over the natural. How it must grieve our Heavenly Father to see the Holy Spirit's work being hampered by human assertiveness and effort. The fact that the anointing oil was not to be put on anyone other than a priest suggests the gifts and graces of the Spirit are for the use of those who belong to God and have entered into covenant with Him. That no simulation was to be made of the oil shows God abhors all efforts to substitute imitations for the genuine ministry of the Holy Spirit.

The nature of fire is to consume and we often use fire to burn away rubbish and impurities. It is fire that purifies lumps of rock into precious metals such as gold and silver (Prov. 17:3; Zech. 13:9). Trials and difficulties purify our faith like gold is purified by fire (1 Peter 1:6–7). Job 23:10 and Malachi 3:3 express similar thoughts. The Spirit will burn away our pride, self-righteousness and bitterness until we are purified and burning with holy zeal.

Other symbols of the Holy Spirit are rain (Hosea 6:3; Joel 2:23), wine (Acts 2:1–21; Eph. 5:18), seal of ownership (2 Cor. 1:22) and a deposit (Eph. 1:13–14). The symbolism of rain is similar to water, although some commentators make much of the fact that the outpouring of the Spirit at Pentecost which soaked and saturated the Church was similar in type to the winter rains. They believe the Church can expect another great outpouring of the Spirit – the 'spring rains' which will prepare it to go out into the world and reap the final harvest. Wine speaks of joy (Eph. 5:18–20; Psa. 104:15) and a deposit as a pledge and guarantee that what we receive here on earth will be multiplied a million times in eternity (2 Cor. 5:5).

Week 5: The Fruit of the Holy Spirit

Opening Icebreaker

There is no great theological truth to this icebreaker! It is merely designed to encourage people to think about fruit and the many varieties of fruit God has introduced into His world.

Bible Readings

Several readings have been given referring in general to spiritual fruitfulness and Christian virtues. It may be helpful to refer to other passages which explain or give examples of those qualities, eg: love in 1 Corinthians 13, Romans 5:8, 1 John 4:10; humility in John 13:1–17, Philippians 2:1–11, Mark 10:42–45 and so on.

Aim of the Session

Have you ever considered what is God's chief goal for your life? It is to mould you into the image of His Son. I like the way the Living Bible paraphrases Romans 8:29, 'For from the very beginning God decided that those who came to him ... should become like his Son.' Isn't that beautiful? And the Holy Spirit has come within you in order to contribute to that great goal. How does He achieve such a tremendous task? By dispersing in our personalities the ingredients of Christ's nature, which Paul describes as the 'fruit of the Spirit'. It is part of the Holy Spirit's role to diffuse and develop this fruit in the hearts and lives of Christ's disciples.

It is vitally important to emphasise that the fruit of the Spirit is not something that is achieved or manufactured but something that is experienced as we abide in Christ and allow the Spirit to produce in us the qualities of Christ's character. That is not to say that we adopt an attitude of passivity in this process, but we actively seek the Holy Spirit's wisdom and help in the various situations we encounter in our lives. Fruit is something that develops and grows as naturally as the plant turns its face to the sun and seeks out water with its roots. As we turn to the Son of God and drink the water of the Holy Spirit, the written word will become a fruitful living Word in our lives. It may be helpful to refer to the parable of the sower in which Christ taught that the nature of the soil was vital in determining the fruitfulness of the seed. The soil cannot produce fruit by itself, but weeds of anxiety, thorns of materialism, shallow roots of commitment and attacks of persecution can choke the good seed that God sows in our hearts (see Mark 4:1–20).

Faithfulness and a desire to obey God even in small things is an important element if we are to be fruitful. Over the years I have seen many promising young people come to faith in Christ and have thought, 'There is a person with a great future in the things of God.' Yet time and time again, I have seen them fail in their faithfulness to little responsibilities or small obligations. Unless there are great changes, that person will end up like the children of Israel in the wilderness – going round and round in circles.

Is fruit an attitude or an action? Really it is both – and in that order. It was the attitude of love that led to Christ's action of sacrificing Himself for us. It was His compassion that caused Him to heal the sick and feed the 5,000. Action without the correct attitude is merely like clanging cymbals, but true fruitfulness is shown when the Spirit-inspired attitude in our hearts leads us to Spirit-powered action with our words and deeds.

Week 6: The Gifts of the Holy Spirit

Opening Icebreaker

Gifts are given not earned and we do not earn spiritual gifts, they are given by the Holy Spirit regardless of our past or worthiness to receive them. Both faithful Stephen and murderous Paul were given the gift of healing. Gifts are only truly valued when they are unwrapped and used! How absurd to be given a computer but never unwrap or use it. It would be tantamount to insulting the giver. Yet as Christians we may sometimes be in danger of not using the gifts and talents that the Holy Spirit has given us.

Bible Readings

Depending on the time available, try to look up and read some of the other references given in the notes.

Aim of the Session

The aim of this session is to explore the gifts of the Spirit. This is not just an academic exercise, however, but an encouragement for people to experience the gifts for themselves.

To emphasise the supernatural does not mean that we automatically devalue human learning, education, natural talents and personal skills. God uses these too. However, we cannot possibly hope to meet the demands made upon the Church unless we know something of a supernatural force and power in our midst. It is as all the members of the Body exercise spiritual gifts that the Church is built up to realise its full potential and proclaim Jesus effectively to the world.

Sometimes gifts may operate together at the same time. One obvious example would be tongues and inter-pretation. It may also be helpful to provide examples of the operation of various spiritual gifts. The *gift of healing* (Acts 3:1–8), a *word of knowledge* (Acts 5:1–5), *discerning of spirits* (Acts 8:18–23) and *miracles* (Acts 9:40). The *discerning of spirits* and *miracles* (Acts 13:8–11) and *words of wisdom* (Acts 16:6–10). The *gift of encouraging prophecy* (Acts 4:36; 9:26–27; 11:22–26) and *predictive prophecy* (Acts 11:27–29).

Be sensitive to any who may have problems with any of the gifts, eg, tongues, healing or the discerning of spirits. Be prepared to talk and pray with them.

Much of the teaching on spiritual gifts centres only on the nine gifts in 1 Corinthians 12:7–10 and yet we read of many other gifts in both that chapter and elsewhere in the Scriptures. Verse 28 specifies 'those with gifts of administration' and it appears that some gifts have a very practical day-to-day application. Although the nine gifts are independent of human faculties, it does seem that the Holy Spirit will take our natural abilities, talents and acquired skills and then supernaturally magnify them for God's glory. The story of Bezalel and skilled craftsmen used to construct the tabernacle is most instructive in this regard (Exod. 36:1–2). Similarly, Huram-Abi used his training and experience to help build Solomon's temple (2 Chron. 2:13–14). Our place and role in the Body of Christ may therefore be related to our natural abilities. For example, those who play instruments to lead worship would normally have a 'good ear', training and considerable practice. It is unlikely that the Spirit would use someone who had never played an instrument before, but rather would come upon a trained musician. We must not rely on our natural abilities, however, but dedicate them to the Lord and seek His supernatural anointing upon them. It is suggested that as we seek and use spiritual gifts we ourselves become a gift to the Body of Christ as God appoints people to ministries in the Church (1 Cor. 12:28; Eph. 4:11).

Week 7: The Spirit-Filled Life

Opening Icebreaker
This should encourage people to reflect on how important it is for every Christian to have a close relationship with the Holy Spirit and stimulate their appetites to desire more of the Spirit on a daily basis.

Bible Readings
Luke 11:11–13 shows how keen God is to give the Holy Spirit to those who ask Him. However, we may put out the Holy Spirit's fire by refusing to offer ourselves fully to Him and accept His ministry. Proverbs 26:20 says, 'Without wood a fire goes out.'

Aim of the Session
The aim of this session is to encourage people to reach out in prayer to God to be filled with the Spirit on a daily basis. The Spirit longs that we might know God by His revelation, glorify God by His fruit, manifest God through His gifts and receive strength from God through His presence in our lives.

Have you ever got excited over a word? Well, let me tell you about one of the most exciting words in the Greek language. It is the word translated 'help' in Romans 8:26 – 'the Spirit helps us in our weakness'. It is actually a combination of three words: *sun* – 'along with', *anti* – 'on the opposite side' and *lambano* – 'to take hold of'. Put them all together and you have the Greek word that reads *sunantilambanotai*. One Greek scholar says it means: 'to take hold of, together with us, over on the other side'. This throws a new and illuminating light on the work and ministry of the Spirit in our lives. The words of Jesus in John's Gospel could be paraphrased thus: 'I will send you a helper who comes alongside when you call, and who will take hold of any burden or problem and carry it with you.' He is with us to take hold of and help us carry our infirmities, our weaknesses, our heavy loads and give us the comfort we need. The Greek experts tell us that the more technically we look at the word, the more exciting it becomes. It is in the indicative mood and represents a fact. It is in the middle voice, indicating that the Holy Spirit is doing the action only with our co-operation and it is in the present continuous tense, speaking of continuous action. He is always there!

The fact that the Holy Spirit is given through Jesus means we need never be afraid to open ourselves to divine power. I have met many Christians who told me they were afraid to ask for the Spirit's power in case they became unbalanced or too emotional and exuberant. The Spirit will always act the way Jesus would act and therefore we can always be confident that like Jesus we can remain balanced, sane and poised and at the same time possess a deep joy and power that can turn the world upside down!

There is much, much more that could be said about the Holy Spirit, but let me close by drawing your attention to something I have emphasised time and time again – *God is willing to give you as much of His Spirit as you are willing to receive.* Encourage each other to seek Him afresh today, that He might flow through your life in the fullness of His power. And don't just focus on being filled for the blessing you might enjoy. Remember, the Holy Spirit is like electricity – He won't come in unless He can get out. Tell Him you want to be a channel, not just a consumer and today will be not an end, but a beginning.

You could conclude the session by praying for people to be filled with the Holy Spirit today and every day.

National Distributors

UK: (and countries not listed below)
CWR, Waverley Abbey House, Waverley Lane, Farnham, Surrey GU9 8EP.
Tel: (01252) 784710 Outside UK (44) 1252 784710

AUSTRALIA: CMC Australasia, PO Box 519, Belmont, Victoria 3216.
Tel: (03) 5241 3288

CANADA: Cook Communications Ministries, PO Box 98, 55 Woodslee Avenue, Paris,
Ontario Tel: 1800 263 2664

GHANA: Challenge Enterprises of Ghana, PO Box 5723, Accra.
Tel: (021) 222437/223249 Fax: (021) 226227

HONG KONG: Cross Communications Ltd, 1/F, 562A Nathan Road, Kowloon.
Tel: 2780 1188 Fax: 2770 6229

INDIA: Crystal Communications, 10-3-18/4/1, East Marredpally, Secunderabad – 500 026.
Tel/Fax: (040) 7732801

KENYA: Keswick Books and Gifts Ltd, PO Box 10242, Nairobi.
Tel: (02) 331692/226047 Fax: (02) 728557

MALAYSIA: Salvation Book Centre (M) Sdn Bhd, 23 Jalan SS 2/64,
47300 Petaling Jaya, Selangor.
Tel: (03) 78766411/78766797 Fax: (03) 78757066/78756360

NEW ZEALAND: CMC Australasia, PO Box 36015, Lower Hutt.
Tel: 0800 449 408 Fax: 0800 449 049

NIGERIA: FBFM, Helen Baugh House, 96 St Finbarr's College Road, Akoka, Lagos.
Tel: (01) 7747429/4700218/825775/827264

PHILIPPINES: OMF Literature Inc, 776 Boni Avenue, Mandaluyong City.
Tel: (02) 531 2183 Fax: (02) 531 1960

REPUBLIC OF IRELAND: Scripture Union, 40 Talbot Street, Dublin 1.
Tel: (01) 8363764

SINGAPORE: Armour Publishing Pte Ltd, Block 203A Henderson Road,
11–06 Henderson Industrial Park, Singapore 159546.
Tel: 6 276 9976 Fax: 6 276 7564

SOUTH AFRICA: Struik Christian Books, 80 MacKenzie Street,
PO Box 1144, Cape Town 8000.
Tel: (021) 462 4360 Fax: (021) 461 3612

SRI LANKA: Christombu Books, 27 Hospital Street, Colombo 1.
Tel: (01) 433142/328909

TANZANIA: CLC Christian Book Centre, PO Box 1384, Mkwepu Street, Dar es Salaam.
Tel/Fax: (022) 2119439

USA: Cook Communications Ministries, PO Box 98, 55 Woodslee Avenue,
Paris, Ontario, Canada.
Tel: 1800 263 2664

ZIMBABWE: Word of Life Books, Shop 4, Memorial Building,
35 S Machel Avenue, Harare.
Tel: (04) 781305 Fax: (04) 774739

For email addresses, visit the CWR website: www.cwr.org.uk
CWR is a registered charity – number 294387

Trusted
All Over the World

Daily Devotionals

Books and Videos

Day and Residential Courses

Counselling Training

Biblical Study Courses

Regional Seminars

Ministry to Women

CWR have been providing training and resources for Christians since the 1960s. From our headquarters at Waverley Abbey House we have been serving God's people with a vision to help apply God's Word to everyday life and relationships. The daily devotional *Every Day with Jesus* is read by over three-quarters of a million people in more than 150 countries, and our unique courses in biblical studies and pastoral care are respected all over the world.

For a free brochure about our seminars and courses or a catalogue of CWR resources please contact us at the following address:

CWR,
Waverley Abbey House,
Waverley Lane,
Farnham,
Surrey GU9 8EP

Telephone: 01252 784700
Email: mail@cwr.org.uk
Website: www.cwr.org.uk

 CRUSADE FOR WORLD REVIVAL   *Applying God's Word to everyday life and relatic*

Cover to Cover Bible Study Guides

These Bible guides from the *Cover to Cover* series, have been created to provide a unique resource for group and individual study lasting between one and two hours. Seven stimulating sessions in each book, supported by opening icebreakers, Bible references, discussion starters and suggestions for personal application.

The Image of God
His Attributes and Character
ISBN: 1-85345-228-9

The Tabernacle
Entering into God's Presence
ISBN: 1-85345-230-0

The Uniqueness of our Faith
What makes Christianity Distinctive?
ISBN: 1-85345-232-7

Ruth
Loving Kindness in Action
ISBN: 1-85345-231-9

Mark
Life as it is Meant to be Lived
ISBN: 1-85345-233-5

Ephesians
Claiming your Inheritance
ISBN: 1-85345-229-7

£3.49 each

The Kingdom
Studies from Matthew's Gospel
ISBN: 1-85345-251-3

The Letter to the Romans
Good news for everyone
ISBN: 1-85345-250-5

The Covenants
God's promises and
their relevance today
ISBN: 1-85345-255-6

Joseph
The power of forgiveness
and reconciliation
ISBN: 1-85345-252-1

Great Prayers of the Bible
Applying them to our lives today
ISBN: 1-85345-253-X

The Holy Spirit
Understanding and experiencing Him
ISBN: 1-85345-254-8

£3.49 each